Azure Wind

Azure Wind

✦

Lessons for Ministry
from Under Sail

Dave Wasserman

iUniverse, Inc.

New York Lincoln Shanghai

Azure Wind
Lessons for Ministry from Under Sail

iUniverse books may be ordered through booksellers or by contacting:

iUniverse
2021 Pine Lake Road, Suite 100
Lincoln, NE 68512
www.iuniverse.com
1-800-Authors (1-800-288-4677)

ISBN-13: 978-0-595-40512-1 (pbk)
ISBN-13: 978-0-595-84880-5 (ebk)
ISBN-10: 0-595-40512-6 (pbk)
ISBN-10: 0-595-84880-X (ebk)

Printed in the United States of America

Contents

In Appreciation

Some say the best sailors are self-sufficient. They need to know everything about their boat's systems. They should carry all the spare parts they could ever need because they know they can't rely on anyone else if the boat falls into trouble. In today's world, good sailors must also be diesel mechanics, electrical engineers, sailmakers, plumbers, carpenters and computer experts.

I disagree. It takes a village to raise a child. It takes a network to make a sailor. Even single-handed sailors need a support team. Joshua Slocum, the first person to sail alone around the world, found a support system every time he put into a port for food and supplies.

It was a very special community that made my sabbatical adventure in the Spring of 2006 such a milestone in my life. Thank you, first, to the leaders and staff of Grace Presbytery, who made my twelve week leave of absence possible. This sabbatical has been such a gift. A special thanks is due to Clark Williams, who served as the Acting General Presbyter during my absence. More importantly, my thanks to the outstanding members of the staff who, through their gifts and commitment, made sure my time away was hardly noticed!

Added to this are the people who sailed with me: my children, Matt, Nick, and Kate Wasserman; friends of thirty years, Peter and Donna Sword; and crew members Kevin Churchill, John Rose, Brian Treybig, Bob Valliere and my colleague in ministry, Dave

VanDam. The cruising community I met in Isla Mujeres, Mexico included Bill and Susie on *Skol*, Steve and Kate on *Santij*, John and Betty on *Second Wind*, and O.D. and Judy on *Cloudwalker*. I am grateful to my Uncle Bud (Ronal Whyte) who introduced me to sailing and to Jerry and Mary Smart, and Earl and Jean Christman who shared their boats and encouraged my interest.

Friends and colleagues who read the early drafts of these reflections were Stan Ott, Dale Patterson, Barbara Ryle, Fred Ryle, and Sheryl Taylor; and Gwen Payne was a great help with administrative assistance, as always.

Finally, to Marney, my wife of thirty-four years and sailing partner: thank you for every encouraging word, for your wordsmithing and editing. Marney spoke our truth when she once wrote: "We have a simple understanding in our marriage. The houses are mine, the boats are his. He's in charge of adventure, I'm in charge of roots." Without her roots, this adventure would never have happened.

dhw

Introduction

In the Spring of 2006, I was granted a three-month sabbatical from my ministry as General Presbyter of Grace Presbytery, a regional office of the Presbyterian Church (USA). I chose to use this time for an active adventure coupled with time for reading and reflecting on thirty-two years of ministry. I planned to sail from Galveston, Texas to Isla Mujeres, Mexico and then farther south to Belize, Guatemala and the Roatan Islands of Honduras.

Like waves rolling into shore and then out again, I've been sailing on and off throughout my life. This particular adventure began in July, 2004 when my wife and I purchased a thirty-one foot sloop, an Island Packet yacht built in 1986 which we named *Azure Wind*. Over the next eighteen months I made thirty-six trips to Kemah, Texas on Galveston Bay from our home in Flower Mound (Dallas/Ft. Worth area) to ready the boat and myself. This would be the most challenging sail I'd ever taken.

On February 28 (the day before Ash Wednesday), three of us left Galveston for Isla Mujeres. Isla lies 650 miles southeast but by the time the winds and current had their way, we traveled closer to 750 miles in seven days. In comparison to the ride home later, the crossing south was an easy sail with only one night of heavy winds.

In its nearly twenty years under previous owners, *Azure Wind* had never traveled off shore. By the end of the first week, her "shakedown" cruise had exposed a series of problems. After several days of repair work, only one problem persisted: a worn mainsail that was becoming impossible to replace. When we finally realized that it would take four to six weeks to have a new one made, I decided to stay in Isla rather than continue farther south and then return home on the repaired main. It was a good decision.

For five weeks I joined the cruising community in Isla. Some of us stayed on the dock, others stayed at anchor. Each day, we talked on the radio and each week, we met for a few social gatherings. I made new friends and learned about the international community of sailors and some of their stories. I learned about the routines of the cruising life, of how you conserve precious resources. I played my guitar, read Scripture, wrote in my journal. I had days alone and time with my children and those friends who were able to adjust their travels to find me on this wonderful island off the Yucatan peninsula.

On April 9 (Palm Sunday), a new crew joined me to make the crossing home. The return ride would take just over five days.

What might the seas offer to those of us making home on land? What can we learn about living from those who go cruising? What can the sailing community share with the community of faith? At first glance, there might seem a disconnect. Those who live on the docks don't often find their way into the church. Just like so many others in our culture.

Yet I discovered insights I hope to hold for the rest of my ministry, lessons about living, fundamentals about the relationships God would have for us with each other and with the creation. Fifteen reflections on my journey follow. The appendices fill in a few of the chronological details, including a copy of the weather forecast we used for the return passage.

With gratitude to God and a humble heart, I invite you to sing a hymn and ride the seas…

Dave Wasserman
Flower Mound, Texas
July, 2006

To Begin

Eternal Father, Strong to Save
1860 and 1861
8.8.8.8.8.8
William Whiting and John Bacchus Dykes

Eternal Father, strong to save, whose arm has bound the restless wave,
Who bade the mighty ocean deep its own appointed limits keep:
O hear us when we cry to Thee for those in peril on the sea.

O Savior, whose almighty word the wind and waves submissive heard,
Who walked upon the foaming deep, and calm amid its rage did sleep:
O hear us when we cry to Thee for those in peril on the sea.

O Holy Spirit, who did brood upon the chaos wild and rude,
And bade its angry tumult cease, and gave, for fierce confusion peace:
O hear us when we cry to Thee for those in peril on the sea.

O Trinity of love and power, all travelers guard in danger's hour;
From rock and tempest, fire and foe, protect them wheresoe'er they go;
Thus evermore shall rise to Thee glad praise from air and land and sea.

Thanks be to God who remembers all who ride life's seas.

1

Leaving Shore

Eternal Father, strong to save,
Whose arm has bound the restless wave,

February 28 was the day *Azure Wind* left shore for its voyage south. I remember thinking how much she looked like a gypsy wagon. The dinghy had been deflated, folded, wrapped in a blue tarp, and placed on a home-made frame located beneath the boom and over the hatch of the main cabin. Eight purple lines lashed it down. The stern pulpit had several contraptions attached to it: a wind generator, a cooking grill, an outboard motor and a can of gasoline. The cockpit was covered with a bimini made of dark blue canvas, reminiscent of the horse-drawn prairie schooners that once traveled the west. And along both walkways leading to the bow were red, five-gallon jerry cans, filled with diesel fuel. They were lashed to boards that had been attached to the stanchions holding the life lines.

Cruising boats heading out to sea can have a comical look to them. It's more the look of a floating contraption than a sleek sailing vessel. So it was for us on February 28th.

Boats are made to leave shore. I spent a year and a half getting ready for this voyage. Twice a month, I drove six hundred miles to the marina for two to three days of work. Those visits, primarily to work on the list of projects, always included a sail in Galveston Bay. Too many boats seldom leave the shore. I saw boats that were beaten up by neglect and ultraviolet damage from the sun that never loosed their lines from the dock. They just stayed put, rocking in the wake of other boats and rotting. Too bad.

Sailors reorient their lives when their boats leave shore. New things become important, like keeping your balance, like listening to the VHF radio and not the CD player, like not falling overboard, like watching the sky, like searching for the ripples in the water that tell you when and where the wind is coming. Leaving shore means gaining your sea legs, facing moments of nausea and, on a passage, learning to live through each day under the constant movement of your boat. In good seas, there's nothing better than the rhythm of a boat, sails trimmed, gliding through the water at its hull speed (the maximum possible speed a boat can travel based on the length of the hull at the waterline). There's a synchronicity to a sailboat moving through the water.

To travel by boat requires a bit of courage and trust that you can face whatever develops. Trust in yourself and your crew's skills, as well as those who have built and maintained the boat. But with the right tools and right heart, leaving shore takes you to places and experiences you'd never reach any other way.

The church is fortunate to have been birthed in a time of sailing. The fishing vessels in Jesus' time were sailboats. The church's first apostles traveled throughout the eastern Mediterranean by sail. And one of the enduring symbols of the church is the sailboat. The symbol suggests that the church is at its best when it is moving on the water, riding the waves, watching the winds, seeking new places to land, new people to meet, new opportunities to learn about God's world from a different anchorage.

Unfortunately, too many congregations can't seem to embrace the sailing perspective. They are like boats tethered to shore, unwilling to release the dock lines, haul up the fenders and head out on the water. They get stuck in stale-looking marinas where there is too little activity. They have too many boat owners in their pews who like to visit on the weekend, look around to make sure everything is secure, maybe tug at a line or two. They may board the boat to sit in the cockpit and have a drink at sunset (or cup of coffee at fellowship hour), pleased with themselves that "all is right with the church and the world," but they don't ever head out into the open water.

They miss the point: sailboats are meant to leave shore. And they miss the adventure of new discoveries and new opportunities. For me, this voyage has been a reminder that all of our planning for a more faithful future in the church is for nothing if we never let go, leave shore and head out. Like the shoe commercial reminds us, sometimes in life, faith, and ministry we need to take a deep breath and "just do it." So be it.

2

Flexibility

I am a planner. I have learned to think ahead, to anticipate, to consider various options and possibilities and to make choices that meet a goal. I've planned programs, workshops, meetings, fund-raisers and construction projects. When I began planning for my sabbatical, I brought those same skills to the table.

For eighteen months I had been working toward a sabbatical that was to include an active adventure, sailing, and a reflective experience, reading and writing. I wanted to do this with friends and family and I knew that I would have to organize and plan for this moment with great care. I looked up charts and measured miles and averaged boat speeds, based on the reading I was doing.

My initial dream was to sail and sail and sail—from Galveston to Panama and the San Blas Islands and back (Mexico, Belize, Honduras, Nicaragua, Panama)—in twelve weeks. Then I re-calculated the distances and made a schedule to Honduras and back (Mexico, Belize, Guatemala, Honduras), approximately 1,100 miles each way. I created eight segments for this voyage (voyage sounds so much better than trip, so much more nautical, but everyone keeps asking about my "trip", sigh). I maximized my time for each segment and minimized the breaks in between. I recruited my crew and by the end of December, 2005, two months before my departure, I had the schedule in place—on paper. Then I was challenged about the "down" time between segments: too short. So I readjusted the schedule. I figured that if the crew needed to sit at the dock for a day or two while some repair was being completed, that would be OK. We'd just have to sail a bit harder to make the next destination. So all was in place, and ready on February 28 when we set sail.

Then the fun began.

It took us seven days to cross the Gulf of Mexico. No problem, I had planned for nine days. However, *Azure Wind* was not holding up so well. Though twenty years old, this was its maiden voyage. By the time we reached Isla Mujeres, we had water pressure problems. We had battery problems. We had a mainsail problem. Within twenty four hours of arriving, we had more issues to add to the list—the fuel line had a small leak somewhere and the bilge was full of water and oil. Now if there's one thing a planner does fairly well, it is to make lists. My repair list kept growing in those first few days. I'd fix one thing and then notice something new—or two somethings new. For all my efforts, the list kept growing.

I was distressed because my carefully planned schedule was collapsing. After four days of repair work, the biggest problem remaining was the mainsail. We had patched the main with sailtape and cloth strips, and then went searching for a used replacement sail. We found one on the internet and made arrangements to have it brought south with the next crew. But when we laid it out, it didn't fit. It was a racing sail not a cruising sail. So my son took it back with him,…and then we learned that to have a new sail made would take four to six weeks.

That's when it occurred to me: the lesson God is offering is flexibility. For all of the planning, I needed to stay flexible. Go with the flow.

Relax. Let it be. Make the decision to deal with what you're dealt. And I did. There was disappointment, but it was mixed with feelings of success, too. I'd just crossed the Gulf of Mexico and was making the safe decision not to go farther south where it would have been even more difficult to face the total loss of a sail. After a couple of day-sails in Cancun bay, I knew I could nurse the patched main back to Galveston. Which is what we eventually did.

In the meantime, I had five great weeks in Isla.

In the church, too often we want the reassurance that our plans will not fail. Our efforts to nurture discipleship and equip people to be sent into the world to serve others, to expand the community and fellowship with new members, to grow the budget all come with the unspoken expectation that good planning won't fail us. The problem happens when we try to plan more than one step at a time. There are no three-step, or nine-step or twelve-step programs for changing the church. There is vision and planning that takes us to the next step and…. flexibility to adjust to emerging realities.

The sailors who get in trouble are the ones who make their plans and can't adjust to the unpredictable weather patterns, mechanical failures, and changes in the human spirit. The ones who survive on the water learn the lesson of flexibility, dealing with what they're dealt.

Just like the palm tree that is pliable enough to bend in the storm force winds, church leaders serve best when they are strong enough to commit to some plan and flexible enough to adjust that plan as needed. God may be in the planning, but God is also in the flexibility.

3

Fear

O Trinity of love and power,
All travelers guard in danger's hour,

I remember the Tuesday we left Kemah and Clear Lake for Isla Mujeres. There had been a growing knot in my stomach. It had been building since the Saturday before. I was deeply afraid of setting out on this voyage. The night before, it took some effort not to panic in front of my wife, Marney (I suspect she saw it in me anyway). "What am I doing? I don't need to do this. I've told my friends and family and my church that I wanted to sail across the Gulf of Mexico but now I'm right on the brink of setting out, and I must be crazy." I held Marney's hand on and off through the night, and I remember praying silently at one point, "Please, God, let me see her again."

The fear was in the anticipation of doing something so very different in my life's journey. The fear was sailing in unknown waters, some that would be thousands of feet deep; the fear was leaving too much of my life behind (friends, family, work, home), of falling overboard, of losing my life. The fear wasn't real, because I wasn't being threatened that night. I was safe at the dock, still tied to land, having yet to depart. It's not like the fear of being in the middle of the water, in the middle of a storm, watching the seas rise and fall and feeling your safety threatened. There were two occasions during the crossings—one each way—when the winds did pick up and we were being roughly tossed about in ten foot seas, yet I wasn't afraid in those moments.

At one point during this time away, a friend read a passage written by Henri Nouwen to the effect that to live is to let go of the regrets from the past and to let go of the worries about the future in order to see the presence of God in the moment, in the present. Something like that. Let go of the regrets (the gift of forgiveness), let go of the worries (the gift of trust), in order to live fully in the moment.

I slept fitfully the night before we left. I woke early and quietly went through the morning routines. I felt a bit numb as I prepared the boat to leave...taking off canvas, setting the jib lines, idling the engine, waiting for the crew to arrive. I didn't feel the anticipated joy of starting a journey I had been planning for over eighteen months. I simply kept going. I guess I was trusting that God had been in the planning and that I needed to keep moving and not turn back.

Within minutes, literally, of leaving the dock, I forgot about the fear. I was busy paying attention to the boat and the water and the breezes as we motored out of the marina, into Clear Lake, then Galveston Bay. Five hours later when we finally reached the Gulf of Mexico, I discovered the joy I had hoped would accompany this time. Still in sight of land, but on our way south.

I've known other fearful moments, some of them real and others imagined. It's the imagined ones that are so debilitating. The real ones can be faced, addressed. We can adjust our sails or our lives to ease those real moments, to restore enough calm to think and act with more clarity. The imagined ones are harder to face, especially when there is no faith to bear its witness in our lives. Forgiveness and trust that lead to a recognition of the present reality of God and the hope offered in Jesus Christ. That kind of faith.

It goes without saying that the church and its people probably have both real and imagined fears about this time in history. Fears about survival, fears about relevance in a culture that seems lost in its own gratification and success, fears about strained relationships and controversies and change and holding on. Some are real; others imagined. The real ones can be faced because we are the people of God, gifted and talented to address, by God's grace, just about anything. The imagined ones must be named for what they are—imagined. Face them with faith.

4

Stewardship

Let's see: the refrigerator uses four to six amps per hour in the charging mode and three to four amps per hour in the standby mode. The autopilot uses four amps per hour, or forty-eight amps every day. The GPS and radar use three amps. Cabin lights, one amp. All told, we used eighty-four amps during the daytime and one-hundred twenty at night. One of the things I discovered is how measured life is on a boat.

You measure your fuel consumption: an hour of motoring at five knots uses four tenths of a gallon. One gallon will keep you moving at five knots for two and a half hours, or twelve-thirteen nautical miles. You calculate: with a twenty-five gallon tank and twenty more gallons in jerry cans on the deck, totaling forty-five gallons times 2.5 hours per gallon times five knots per hour equals somewhere between 500 and 560 miles of motoring or motor sailing.

You measure your water consumption: a sixty gallon tank of fresh water, not including the bottled drinking water brought on board, figuring one gallon of water per day per person (for drinking, bathing, and a share of the cooking and cleaning water needed, but not including water used in the head which is saltwater) gives three gallons a day or enough water for a twenty day trip.

And it can get complicated. We had an old watermaker that made one gallon of fresh water from the salty seawater an hour but used four to six amps which meant that much more time recharging the batteries (at forty amps per hour), which you did by running the engine and consuming diesel fuel!

The cruising life is a measured life. I was surprised by the detailed electrical management that was required on this trip. I was cautious about the fuel and careful about the water. Even in Mexico at the marina where the water pressure in the men's shower was a trickle at best. Even under that slow flow, those were some of the best showers I've ever had.

Cruising sailors learn the lessons of stewardship—of careful management of precious resources. Cruisers don't necessarily attribute those resources to the gracious generosity of God. I do. And God's resources are precious.

Since my return, I have been painfully aware of how much electricity I use. And I'm a product of the energy crisis of the 1970's and still go around turning off every light I can. I'm noticing how much we run our lights and fans and motors and think nothing of what we're doing. And I have been embarrassingly aware of the water pressure coming from my shower and am learning to cut back. We complain about gas prices, but I, for one, could do more to conserve the gasoline I purchase for my truck.

My money is precious to me. I try to spend it carefully and use it wisely. I used my money to have electricity, water and diesel on *Azure Wind*. I spend my money to have these same things at home in Flower Mound, Texas. They are resources for my daily living, as are my food and insurance payments. They are simply the cost of living. I use one resource to secure other resources, all needing to be used carefully and in a measured way.

In a similar way, we do well to consider our pledges and financial support of the church as securing the resources for daily living the faith, not simply for ourselves but for others, too. Participating in a community means that many benefit beyond what we see in our own spheres and circles. We covenant to present and interpret the Scriptures and their mandate to a life of faithful service to God. We can't do it alone, we need each other. It's all about the careful management of precious resources. When ministry nurtures people in the faith and serves those in need, it is a precious gift from God. One that needs to be used carefully and in a measured way.

I didn't expect that my time on *Azure Wind* would heighten my awareness that the stewardship season is 24-7-365. But it is.

5

Keeping Watch

O Holy Spirit, who did brood
Upon the chaos wild and rude,

I know now what I didn't know at the time: that the trip from Galveston to Isla Mujeres is one of the longer voyages that Caribbean cruisers make. It's about 650 miles along the rhumb line, the most direct route. That's about the same distance for sailors traveling from North Carolina to Bermuda. It's about the farthest reach across the Gulf of Mexico and one of the longest stretches sailors will traverse in the Caribbean. Most cruisers make trips that last two to four days. Our journey south was six days and twenty-two hours (five days, fifteen hours on the return). That meant that for seven nights on the first crossing, we had a watch schedule.

I had watch from 9:00—11:00 pm and from 3:00—5:00 am. It's dark, no artificial lights to intrude on the night sky, and on the nights when the winds are gentle and the waves are easy, it's a great experience. Most of the nights we headed south like that. There was one that was not.

That night, the seas were rolling and had grown to eight feet. The winds had picked up to twenty knots and we were heeling (leaning over) to an angle of twenty degrees. Occasionally some wave would splash into the cockpit. To give you an idea of what that night was like, try an experiment with your spouse or a good friend. Have them wake you up at 3:00 am with a sudden nudge saying, "your watch". Then, get out of bed—make sure you're wearing the same gym shorts, t-shirt and socks that you've worn for the last three days. Throw on some sweat pants, a long sleeved warm shirt and then a nylon jacket and knit cap for your head. Finally, add a life vest and harness that weigh about five pounds. Now, go to your bathroom and step into the shower. Make sure you've placed a little stool on the floor and that two of the legs of the stool have been sawed off by several inches. Sit down, turn out all the lights and then have your friend turn on the cold water for a few seconds periodically over the next two hours!

Whether it's a rough night or a calm one, keeping watch involves three tasks. First, you don't fall asleep. Actually, that's one advantage of a rough sea. You're not so likely to drift off, but neither are you likely to get much rest down below. Whatever it takes, rough seas, food, music from an MP3 player, you stay awake. There is less reaction time at night than you might think. You can see three to five miles at the horizon. A light from a ship traveling at fifteen knots heading toward your boat traveling at five knots gives you ten to fifteen minutes to decide if you are on a collision course and if you need to make some course correction. Not a lot of time. You have to stay awake.

Secondly, keeping watch involves actively looking in all directions. Every fifteen minutes, you get up from your seat, sometimes with and sometimes without binoculars, and look for lights on the horizon. If you are in a ship lane you stay very active. If you are out on the open water, you can relax a bit. When you don't have fancy equipment like radar and computer screens that identify all the traffic in the area, you look all around you. Initially, my first watch focused on looking out for the oil and gas rigs in the night. Usually they were well lit, some of them like a small city. And because they were stationary, I focused my attention on what was ahead, not what we'd put behind us. When the boat moved into the shipping lanes, I realized that watch keeping is a three hundred sixty degree task. Your small and slow sailboat is no match for the speeds of a tanker or cruise ship. You can be just as easily overtaken from behind as meet a boat coming across your bow. Unless you know you're the fastest boat on the water, you look in all directions.

Finally, watch keeping involves sensitizing yourself to changing conditions. On virtually every cruising boat, including *Azure Wind*, there are instruments that help you watch the direction and speed of the wind. You look for wind shifts of five degrees or five knots. That's not much, but it is significant enough that you need to alter your course or you will put undue stress on your sails and rigging.

Stay awake. Actively look. Measure the changes.

Now, all kinds of biblical images come to mind. Habbakuk writes of watching from a tower for the Messiah to arrive. Jesus told a parable about keeping watch: the ten maidens waiting for the returning bridegroom, some who went below to refill their lamps and missed the boat, as it were.

For today's church, this is a time to be keeping watch. God is doing something very new as we face the challenge of reshaping denominations and congregations that are not helping fulfill God's mission in our time. Most of us know we are facing sea change. Some are experiencing the churning and chopping waters. Others look away and are becalmed by the complacency of old traditions. A few are sitting back and waiting, holding onto a belief that the winds will eventually shift back and refill our sails on the course we've always traveled.

Regardless, we'd best be about the work of keeping watch. This is not a time to take a nap. We must discipline ourselves to look around. Church leaders need to look behind as well as ahead. They need to affirm the good work of the past and the signs of life that lie ahead. They need to visit other places of worship, ask good questions that can lead to growth, and share best practices with one another. Watch keeping involves a 360 degree view and review.

There's a wonderful Advent hymn that narrates a conversation between a watchman and a traveler. "Watchman tell us of the night," it begins. "Traveler, o'er yon mountain's height."(*) The hymn suggests that some one is watching and some one else is traveling. When you're on a sailboat the two are inseparable. Travelers keep watch. Lookouts ride the waters.

Stay awake. Actively look. Measure the changes. Be well.

(*) Watchman, Tell us of the Night

1825, 1879
John Bowring, Joseph Parry
ABERYSTWYTH 7.7.7.7 D

Watchman, tell us of the night, What its signs of promise are.
Traveler, o'er yon mountain's height, See that glory-beaming star.
Watchman, does its beauteous ray Aught of joy or hope foretell?
Traveler, yes; it brings the day, Promised day of Israel.

Watchman, tell us of the night, Higher yet that star ascends.
Traveler, blessedness and light, Peace and truth its course portends.
Watchman, will its beams alone Gild the spot that give them birth?
Traveler, ages are its own; See, it bursts o'er all the earth.

Watchman, tell us of the night, For the morning seems to dawn.
Traveler, darkness takes its flight, Doubt and terror are withdrawn.
Watchman, let your wanderings cease; Hasten to your quiet home.
Traveler, lo, the Prince of Peace, Lo, the Son of God is come!

6

Boundaries

Who bade the mighty ocean deep
Its own appointed limits keep

Through my sailing experiences I've been reminded of the three basic contexts in God's creation: the land, the sea and the air. And I've found myself curious about the boundaries between them. For example, where land and air meet becomes a setting with great creative or destructive potential. When the fresh air and rains brought by the wind touch the rich earth, the goodness of the harvest comes forth: wheat, corn, soy, vegetables, fruit appear. On the other hand, great destructive forces can engage that same boundary: dust storms and tornadoes, among them.

In similar ways, the boundary between air and water can bring the good winds and seas for sailing, or the stormy hurricanes that lead to so much destruction. The boundary between land and sea can be as dangerous as the rocky shoals and breakwaters or as welcoming as the gentle lapping of a sandy bay. I suspect most of us think of the land/sea boundary in terms of the pristine beach on a deserted island. Check out the screensavers on most of our computers.

On Isla, I found myself thinking about the land/sea boundary a little differently one day. I was off to buy some bottled water for the fresh water tank, ten gallons of it and decided to take the dinghy rather than carrying jerry cans along the road. I motored over to the "RO" plant (Reverse Osmosis) and tied the dinghy to a tree root. I helped pour water from their five gallon containers into my two and a half gallon ones. I paid my twenty-six pesos (twenty-six cents) for the ten gallons. When I returned to the dinghy, I paused for a few minutes and noticed what I normally ignore. There, in front of me, was a mess of human scraps: a tire, the pop tops from some beer cans, old rags, plastic refuse from some discarded container, deteriorating boat lines, three fish-heads, wood pieces from an old and long gone rowboat.

And I watched the gentle battle that seemed to be happening between the sea and the land, the water and the sand. Neither the sea nor the land wanted this refuse, our waste. The sea, with its small waves, kept pushing the junk up onto the shore. The sand, in return, kept dissipating and falling away, trying to give it back. There was almost a politeness about it: "No, you have their stuff;…Oh no, I insist, you take it."

Boundary waters and space can be filled with the junk of our lives. In the church, we tend to think of the boundary waters that way. Our recent experiences related to issues of leadership conduct tend to make us wary of the boundaries. And, we pay attention not to invade someone else's space, to step on someone else's tradition, or program, or institutional preferences. Keep it safe, and simple, and separate. It's risky and messy at the boundaries.

Only it's hard to keep the boundary line so neat and clean. You can't draw that line in the sand and expect it to stay there. It doesn't take long for the sea and sand to make something different of our lines.

So, it's worth remembering that there are good things that happen at the boundaries, too. Shells find a new home in the sand, plants rise through the shallow surface and create strength to keep water and land separate enough to weather storms. The seas wash the shore and the land gives back its richness. And in ministry, the boundary waters can be the place where the best action is found, when the church ministers at the edge of the culture, when people push beyond their stereotypes and build relationships that honor God.

It's worth noticing what happens where air and land and sea meet each other. Like the church mouse, there's probably a few good stories that the shells and rocks and wood and rags could tell, given the chance. And, it wouldn't hurt us one bit to pay a little more attention to the junk we spread along the boundaries in God's world.

7

Danger

From rock and tempest, fire and foe
Protect them whereso'er they go;

The night of Maundy Thursday, 2006 is burned into my memory. Actually it was the very early minutes of Good Friday, just past midnight that we received a call on the VHF radio. The VHF is one of those essentials for boating, and is critical for the nighttime. There is a certain language to learn and a protocol to follow. You never turn off the radio; from the moment of departure to the time of arrival, it stays on because it is a lifeline and part of the safety net.

That evening, another crew member was on watch; I was resting (can't say I was sleeping) in the quarterberth below. The crew member reported later that he had been tracking two sets of bright lights on the horizon, off the left (port) side of the boat. He could see the green bow light which meant that the boat was moving in a crossing pattern toward us. The other set of lights, more distant, were a white blur. He was keeping an eye on both ships.

About 12:30 am, the radio crackled. "This is the CV Aquarius (Commercial Vessel Aquarius) trying to reach the small vessel at 28 degrees, 50 minutes North, and 93 degrees, 55 minutes West, bearing a course of 320 degrees." I immediately slipped out of bed and grabbed the microphone. I called back and identified ourselves as the Sailing Vessel Azure Wind. "Yes, Captain, this is Aquarius and we have you on our radar moving in the direction of another ship, the CV Symphony, which is towing a barge on a 10,000 meter cable. We advise you to make a course correction and (he paused)...let me get Symphony and you can talk directly. Please stand by."

Azure Wind was heading northwest toward Galveston. Symphony was heading northeast toward New Orleans or Mobile.

I looked up at crew member Dave Van Dam on watch who said, "That's us. It's our coordinates and heading." I went up into the cockpit and saw the lights for myself.

Dave and I looked at each other through the shadows. We couldn't believe what we had heard: a 10,000 meter cable. I had heard about long towing cables, but I had not imagined one that was nearly six miles in length. I know about a 10,000 meter mountain, a 10,000 meter race, but I wouldn't have thought anybody would ever use a 10,000 meter cable. Steel, I'm sure. Towing a barge or some very large object, like a drilling rig. Did I say steel cable? Either right at, below, or slightly above the water line. We were on a course that would put us behind the first boat, in front of what we thought was a second boat, smack dab into a cable that would have broken our hull, or taken our mast with a snap. And at night.

In minutes, CV Symphony came on the air and we began the work that saved our lives. Yes, he could see us on his radar. No, our radar was only working at close range and he was past our viewing distance. Yes, he could see that our course was taking us into the cable. No, he was not in a position to alter his course. It wouldn't have done any good anyway because of the slow lag time in turning the barge and cable.

He gave us our choices. Turn slightly southwest and head back towards Mexico for two hours until we were behind the barge. Turn slightly north-northeast and head toward New Orleans for about one hour and pass in front of his vessel. We headed north. We turned on the engine and made arrangements for Symphony to call us again when we were past his vessel and clearly out of harm's way.

The seas remained safe that night because people on the open water understand how much they need each other. It's not just the laws, it's the norms. You look out for danger and you work to avoid catastrophes.

In the church, there are hidden dangers that threaten the fabric of faith and community. They come at us in various ways. Some just below the surface, some just above. A conflict among members or more often, between some members and the expectations about their pastor can undermine momentum in a church's life. In this impatient time when we give head coaches two years to turn the team around or be fired, it's not surprising that our anxiety for quick success can lead to conflict between pastors and leaders and members. Or, what about the confusion some popular book or film creates. The *Left Behind* series or the *da Vinci Code*. When too many Christians use their Bibles as dust collectors and not a foundational source for living, it's not surprising that some fictitious (or partially true) ideas become believable.

These are the kinds of dangers best faced together. We need each other to get through the rough waters: we need conservatives and liberals, old and young, rich and poor. We need the people who sit in the pews and attend the national church meetings. We need people from other parts of the world as well as our neighbors at home. We need each other to pass through the troubled waters of life in the church.

I suspect that the longer we live, the more we're inclined to think we've seen it all. Or enough so that there are few surprises left for us to discover. Not in the wee hours of Good Friday, 2006. With the help of some passing friends, I survived one more surprise in my life's journey. Ten thousand meters!

8

Passagemaking

O Savior, whose almighty word
The wind and waves submissive heard

My first experiences of sailing were on small racers and day sailers. My uncle Bud raced a wooden Snipe 16 on Indian Lake in northwest Ohio. His son and daughters were the primary crew, but each summer when I spent a week with my cousins, I would be invited to take a sail. We would be on the water for a few (three) hours at most and I enjoyed those times. I picked up sailing again during college because our school had a lake campus and you could earn a PE (Phys. Ed.) credit by taking a sailing class. In our first pastorate in Iowa, we made friends with the owners of a thirty foot sailboat and joined them for a couple of outings. Day sailing was fun. You wake up in your bed, spend time on the water for a couple of hours and return home before the day is done.

In the 1980's during our second pastorate, a new church development in Arizona, Marney and I made friends with an older clergy couple who owned a sailboat in San Diego. Years after we had moved away, we received a phone call one day inviting us to meet them for a weekend of sailing. We accepted the invitation and flew to San Diego. By the end of that weekend, I had found a new passion. I bought all the sailing magazines I could find at the airport newsstand and shortly thereafter signed up for the first of several credentialing courses. Within a month, I had chartered a twenty-six foot sailboat for an afternoon on an Oklahoma lake. Within a year, we had completed our first bareboat charter in the eastern Caribbean. For that one week, two couples daysailed and lived on a 36 foot sloop. We hauled anchor each morning, set sails and went someplace new to set the hook again and grill our dinner off the back of the boat. We cooked our meals, rinsed our bodies and washed our hair, and lived in a 150 square foot space. We saw sunsets, moon rises, night stars and occasionally the sunrise. It was great and the first of many Caribbean charters we would take.

But daysailing, on a lake or on a charter, is not the same as passagemaking. Passagemaking involves overnight sailing. It takes one night to make a passage from Galveston to Corpus Christi. It takes twenty-four days to make a passage from the Canary Islands in the eastern Atlantic to St. Lucia in the eastern Caribbean. It takes five to seven days to make a passage across the Gulf of Mexico, as we discovered on *Azure Wind*.

I sense that many, if not most, cruisers don't like passagemaking. They try to minimize the number of days out on the open water by turning on the engine and motorsailing, or by making shorter passages. Instead of a long passage from Galveston to Isla, many would rather hop-skip along the gulf coast to Key West and sail from there. A seven day passage would be reduced to three. Of the twenty cruisers I met going from the US to Isla, only three came straight across the gulf. The others worked their way to the Florida coast.

Passagemaking is an endurance test. Imagine driving a motor home from northeast Texas to Albuquerque on a gravel road, one that has sections of deep ruts and potholes in it. One that has some twists and turns and restricts your speed to five to seven miles per hour. Northeast Texas to Albuquerque is about the same distance as it was for *Azure Wind's* trip to Isla. You never leave the motor home. It just keeps moving, never stops, you take turns at the wheel even though you have the cruise control turned on. You live in the same clothes, you don't shower, you are in constant motion for everything you experience—cooking, cleaning, using the head, reading, writing, taking pictures. Always in motion.

We discovered that each crew member had his own personal rhythms to attend to. We set a watch schedule for the night sailing. The most sleep any of us had at a stretch was four hours. We ate breakfast on our own and tried to have lunch and supper at the same time, mostly because it took so much effort to prepare sandwiches or cook soup while you were leaned over at ten to fifteen degrees. You take cat naps during the day and after a few days of this, your body adjusts.

Passagemaking requires an endurance that is rare for most of us. Once you start a passage, you can't stop the movement until you reach the shore again. You either make the crossing or you turn back, and if you turn back then you typically have an hour's movement back for each hour you have traveled. At one point on the passage south, I thought about the wisdom of turning back. We had been using so much fuel the first few days that I began to wonder if we had enough remaining to go forward. We decided to wait one more day and thankfully the winds picked up. After that, we knew we'd make it across. We kept going.

There are very few activities that require such endurance from the human body or spirit. Marathon runners come to mind. Long distance swimmers come to mind. So do record setting hot-air balloon pilots. Most of our lives are lived with short bursts of high speed, multi-tasking and fast-fooding along the way.

Endurance is a wonderful gift. In the church, it is necessary because the changes the church is facing will not happen overnight with short bursts of high speed alone. Those moments may be necessary, but they need to be set in the larger context of long-term change. I remember visiting one of the churches in the Presbytery (district) and being challenged by an older gentleman about the issue of homosexuality and church leadership. "Why can't we solve this dilemma? It seems so clear to me." It struck me that he was wanting to go to his grave knowing that a resolution had been found. And I said, "Sir, like everything else, this is happening on God's time, not ours. We can't determine when we will have a resolution. We've been talking and praying about this for twenty-five years. We may need to talk and pray about it for twenty five more." Controversies aside, the bigger challenge I see is changing a church that has been passive in its outreach, to one that nurtures disciples to be active in sharing the faith in their daily lives, one where our bodies and not just our money are offered for God's work and Christ's mission. That's a serious turning for a tradition-laden institution that loves to tell the story of a time when the church grew (1950's in case you've forgotten) by simply unlocking the doors on Sunday mornings.

Just as you don't turn the cruise ship "on a dime", so you won't turn the church toward the "new thing" God is doing and calling us to engage by simply adding a new program for the fall schedule.

I wouldn't want to make a life of passagemaking, but I'm glad for the two long crossings and the endurance lessons they offered.

9

Patience

And bade its angry tumult cease,
And gave, for fierce confusion, peace.

One of the biggest lessons of my trip with *Azure Wind* was about patience. Often cruisers are viewed as having a luxurious, easy-going lifestyle. They live on a well-equipped boat, stay at beautiful anchorages, enjoy the natural rhythms of water and sun. They seem to smile all the time (who wouldn't smile when you're surrounded by all that blue water!) and are seen as easy going, friendly, on a year-round vacation of sorts. Not so. Much of this perception is patience masked.

When I first arrived in Isla, one of the cruisers smiled when he heard about my original plans. I had armchair-planned this voyage as though I were going to be on a cruise liner for twelve weeks. I had mapped the distance between each port, estimated the number of days it would take to sail that distance, and then allowed three to four days for a change of crew and some rest. My new friend said that when meeting people out cruising, you give them one of two choices. "I tell my friends, you can choose where to meet the boat or when to meet the boat, but you can't choose both. If you choose where, I'll tell you when and wait for you. If you choose when, then I'll tell you where I am."

I now understand why cruisers don't entertain much. If they need help in making a two-three day passage, they look for local crew. If they want family or friends to visit, they plan to spend a month in one place and have folks travel to that location. It takes patience with the schedule to host others.

The weather forces a patient posture. I stayed for a little over a month in one place and I was struck by the number of days that, given the weather report, none of the cruisers planned to start their next passage. They look for weather windows. Each day, they review a week of weather forecasts and consider whether a window is developing. They want the winds from the right direction and at tolerable speeds, and they'd prefer not to face rain or storms or strong currents or steep waves along the way. So they wait. They're patient and given the stress of any passage, glad to wait for the best moment to head out.

Boat repairs also demand patience. If you sail a boat, plan on something breaking down. If you bring a supply of spare parts and happen to have the right one with you, consider yourself fortunate. You may be able to make a quick fix, unless you don't know how to fix it yourself. In that case, good luck finding a local, skilled and available mechanic. You can spend a week just locating someone who will come to your boat. On the other hand, if you don't have the spare part, then life really slows down. You have to make contact with a dealer or supplier, most often in the United States, to place an order. And sometimes they'll ship it directly to you and it will be waiting at the nearest airport for you to retrieve it…often paying customs outlandish prices. So, cruisers ask around to see who may be traveling to some nearby boat and wouldn't mind carrying a spare part with them. My sons Nick and Matt carried a main sail when they flew from Dallas to Cancun. Daughter Kate brought engine filters with her for a neighbor's boat. When you're new to cruising, it always takes longer to repair your boat than you think. Patience.

Patience is a spiritual gift. Some of us are more patient than others. The longer we live, the more patient most of us become. Patience is a necessity in sailing, or at least the cruising part of sailing (can't say patience is on the captain's mind in a race). The longer I live, the more I recognize the need for patience in ministry. Changing the culture of a church so that it focuses on outreach, nurture and service (reaching, growing, being sent) does not happen on some preconceived timetable. Like the weather, you wait for the right moment to introduce the next step of change. Like repairs, you serve the church best when you take your time to attend to wounded relationships, or fix communication issues or worship/budget/program dilemmas. It takes more time than we ever think we have.

Good Lord, think about how patient God is with us. A life more patiently lived is a worthy one. In its own way, my voyage was well worth this simple reminder.

10

Community Building

"Welcome to the Isla Mujeres Cruisers' Net. My name is Ted on *Ischabod* and I'll be your net controller." Seven days a week, at 9:00 am, the community network formed on the VHF radio, Channel 13. There was an agenda that went like this: Are there any emergencies? Hearing nothing, we'll move on. Are there any new boats in the harbor? Please identify yourselves, where you came from and how many are on board. Then there was the roll call of boats. Each of us listening would identify ourselves. Next, there was the weather report. Two boats took on the responsibility of downloading weather information from various sources. One of them presented the big picture for the western and eastern gulf, the Yucatan peninsula, Mexico/Belize. The other developed projections of a virtual weather buoy located about 30 miles north of Isla. We listened and took our notes. Then Ted would ask, "All right, given this weather, are there any boats planning to leave within the next twenty-four hours?" On most days I participated on the net, silence followed this question. After pausing, then Ted would go to the remaining part of the agenda: any questions, any announcements, any new discoveries in terms of services or restaurants? He'd ask about any "Treasurers from the Bilge", which was the opportunity to sell or buy other cruiser's junk (er, recyclables). The network closed with a joke of the day. Occasionally, other cruisers filled in for Ted and brought their own personalities to the task, but the agenda remained the same and had an almost liturgical quality to it. During my time in Isla, there were always at least ten and some days as many as twenty boats participating on the morning net.

The cruising community created an identity through this daily radio meeting. Unless they were having an individual conversation on another channel, most cruisers kept their VHFs tuned to 13 throughout the day. When you are on the seas, you keep your radio on Channel 16. When you are in port, official contact with the harbormaster stays on 16. But cruisers find their own home by claiming a different channel that is available for public (not commercial) use. So, I kept my radio on 13 and joined the net—and the community.

Despite the image of self-sufficiency, it's the nature of the cruising community to stay connected, if nothing else than for some attentive ears to listen to your stories or some sympathetic ones to hear about your woes.

I quickly discovered that cruisers will gladly share their skills and talents. If you need help with a sail, you ask around. You'll likely hear the name of someone who has more experience than most and is willing to give some time for an initial look. If you need help with the engine or most anything mechanical or electrical, there is usually someone in the harbor willing to get you started. There are some folks who are so ill-prepared and ill-equipped that they become beggars when they travel. Cruisers will figure this out and learn ways to side-step a developing nuisance. Most of the time though, cruisers will step up to share their information, skills, and occasionally spare parts with someone else. Helping each other is fundamental to the cruising community.

Oddly, some people don't want help when they need it. One day, a catamaran anchored in the harbor dragged its anchor. The boat was old and had lost its mast during Hurricane Wilma in the fall of 2005. The owner, an old man living alone, was something of a hermit and apparently had developed severe diabetes and gangrene on one foot. He refused medical help because, I suspect, he couldn't afford it. The day his boat dragged, four other cruisers, at some risk to themselves, took their dinghies out onto the choppy water to offer assistance. The boat had drifted onto a shoal and was being pushed farther aground. The four were clearly on an errand of mercy because once the boat had drifted past their own boats, they were out of harm's way. They simply wanted to help and tried to talk the old man into letting them do so. He was confused and began swearing at them and, after a while, they motored back to their own boats.

That same day, another sailboat pulled into the anchorage and dragged its anchor. The engine wouldn't start and the two young sailors were desperate for help. Two dinghies and one pontoon boat offered their tow lines and brought the boat to the marina where several more helped secure the dock lines.

It's the nature of the cruising community to help each other through difficulties.

On Friday evenings, subject to weather of course, many in the cruising community gathered for a potluck supper and beers. On Saturday mornings, they met at a restaurant for breakfast. These were important social occasions. If you were hosting friends or family members, you simply brought them along. You put names and faces together (Oh, you're the folks on *Second Wind*). You shared sailing stories and laughed at tall tales. On several Friday nights, our community pulled out the drums, autoharp, guitars, and spoons and sang our way through the 60's and 70's and 80's, and even a bit of the 50's, too. You shared your food, drank a cheap beer, and made merry. And once you put names and faces together, then you'd look for each other as you walked the island buying groceries and supplies or you made your phone calls back to the states.

Fellowship was important because cruisers like to be with each other. Their common interests and commitments keep them looking out for one another.

The cruising community forms and reforms itself all the time. Every old boat that departs and each new boat that arrives changes the community's personality. The routines stay the same. And you leave knowing you may never see someone again. You may end up in the same anchorage or harbor down the coast with one or two boats, but not the entire community. It's not in the nature of cruisers to convoy or caravan.

Networking, helping, gathering. These characteristics are pretty basic to most human communities.

In most congregations we experience all of these: networking, helping, gathering. Better than most institutions, the church knows what it is to be in a covenant relationship with shared values and expectations, one that builds bridges through networking, offers support and encouragement in times of need, and gathers for the important communal work of worship, fellowship, study, service. Congregations that do these well survive the ups and downs of life and ministry. And there is evidence in our denominational structures that we are starting to figure this out: networking, helping, gathering are the hallmarks of both the local and the larger church God is assembling in our time.

I wonder sometimes if this common experience may be more critical to sustaining a community than a common theology or politics or pension plan. Helping each other is more important than who wins. It's worth pausing to consider.

11

Shelling

One of the greatest gifts of my voyage was the opportunity to live at a slower pace. For seven weeks, I traveled no faster than 7–8 miles per hour. On Isla, I walked more than I rode in cabs. I woke with the sun. Actually it was before the sun on many days, because we were docked near a noisy commercial boat that started its huge and very loud diesel engines between 4:30 and 5:00 am. Life slowed: the basics of daily living—eating, washing, etc.—simply took longer. All of it meant that I didn't accomplish a long list of tasks on any day. And, I read and wrote some. All of it slowed me down.

I especially enjoyed the walking. From the marina, I walked south into the Colony, the area of the island where the locals live. My farthest trip was to buy cases of water and beer. I'd walk past the R/O plant (reverse osmosis for turning sea water into drinking water). I walked past the little hardware store with the Quaker State sign on it. I walked past the lunch counter with the foosball table where the kids played after school. I walked past the middle school with the kids in their uniforms. I walked past homes and stores and the Coca Cola plant and the beer distributor.

When I walked north from the marina, I walked along a road that paralleled the small naval airstrip runway toward the commercial district with its restaurants, souvenir shops, travel and day/tour agents, small hotels and governmental offices. I went past hurricane damaged buildings, some homes, a new restaurant under construction, the Mexican Navy's base and dock, and a beach.

For most of my time, I walked with a purpose: to exercise and get something done on my errand list. While I noticed things, I missed many of the details.

Then my wife joined me.

Of the many activities Marney likes to do, shelling is near the top of her list. Whenever we've chartered a boat, her goal isn't the sailing as much as it is reaching an anchorage where there's a good beach. She grew up on Long Island Sound and visited her grandmother each year on Martha's Vineyard. She loves to walk the beaches and look for shells. And when she's around, I enjoy going with her.

So, we went shelling one afternoon. We walked toward town and then detoured off the road to a beach of fine sand and palm trees near the boat anchorage. It was a bright, clear, hot, sunny day. We brought a bottle of water and a plastic bag.

And then we began. Walking very slowly. Almost tiptoeing across the beach. Right at the edge where the water and land meet. Noticing the push and pull of the small waves. Noticing the covering and uncovering of shells with each splash of water. We worked around seaweed and human debris. We noticed the seabirds standing in the shallows ahead of us and slowed our pace so as to not disturb them, though we knew that eventually we would walk too close for their comfort. We relished the breeze that would pick up and cool us for a moment. It was a wonderful moment of noticing and appreciating the details of life, and picking up a few of them to take home.

I don't shell enough on land. I don't slow down to notice the details often enough. I've hurried through too many of my days with my long list of tasks that gets pressured by the numerous interruptions for which I'm paid. I like to plan ahead, think about tomorrow. I worry more than I should about yesterday even though I can't change one thing.

Many years ago, there was a ten-part television series entitled "The Long Search". It was produced by the British Broadcasting System to introduce viewers to the key religions of the world. I remember the segment on Buddhism in which a monk took one hour to walk ten feet (no, the one-hour episode did not consist of a walking monk, but I bet at least five minutes was devoted to watching him!). It was an exercise in the discipline of slowing down and noticing the present. Shelling does that for me.

I confess I like to work through a long list of tasks. It makes me feel that I'm making a contribution to something greater than myself. I'm helping someone by listening to him or her, sitting in a meeting, writing a letter of recommendation, guiding a decision. We live in a culture that values this fast-paced, multi-tasking life. The name "*fast* food" is no accident.

I think about the church and sometimes wish it worked a bit faster. It takes forever to call a new pastor. Building a building takes longer than you ever expect. Changing the order of worship happens best when it happens slowly most times. Maybe there's something to slow-paced change that I need to appreciate. Maybe it's more enduring. Maybe the church is right to take its changes slowly. It's hard to see this in the world we live in.

Frankly, the longer I live, the more I'm interested in shelling. My instincts tell me to follow this one.

12

Planning

*Thus evermore shall rise to Thee
Glad praise from air and land and sea.*

Have I mentioned that I am a planner? Ask anyone who has worked with me and they'll confirm that I do this a lot. I guess I believe God is in the planning as much as the doing; God is in the future as much as the present. I remember a minister introducing his prayer at the memorial service for a colleague by saying, "I believe God's Spirit is in the moment, but my prayer today has been written out. So, in the belief that God's Spirit was in the writing as much as in the speaking, let us pray:…"

From the moment we took possession of *Azure Wind* in July 2004, I had been planning to make this voyage (did I say "trip"?). I needed more experience to gain confidence in my sailing and I needed the time to work out the details for such an extended trip. So, I began planning.

I planned for the boat's improvements. I made lists of all the things that would be needed to make this boat as seaworthy as possible: new lines, new winches, new bottom paint, new batteries. I made lists of some safety items I would want: replacing a life line, new life jackets and harnesses, new jack lines, a life raft, an EPIRB (emergency distress signal radio beacon), a suture kit and inflatable splints. I made lists of ongoing maintenance work that would need to be done: regular scrubbing of the hull, oiling the teak, polishing the stainless steel. I made lists of the communication equipment and programs I'd want to have: a navigation program for the laptop, a satellite telephone, cables to connect the computer to the phone and to my handheld GPS, all to make sure I could stay in contact while I was sailing. And I kept a schedule of it all—when I did what, who I employed and what it cost.

I was making myself ready and even though I suspected that there would be some surprises, I figured they'd be minor rather than major.

It was exciting and exhilarating as I did all this preparation work. As the day of departure approached, the excitement was mixed with growing anxiety. Had I thought of everything important? What was I missing? What could I still do before my departure date?

Planning is good, but it only works if you can stay flexible about your plans. By definition, you can't be certain about the surprises. Planning can be a source of pride, but it needs to be approached in humility (and good humor).

Ministry is no different than a sailing voyage. God is in the planning as much as in the moment. If you don't plan well for Vacation Bible School or a summer mission trip, it will show and could be harmful to someone. If you assume that the details you addressed at last year's Christmas pageant will serve you for this year's version, you may miss something important. If you ignore the emotions involved in asking people to change their outlook and behaviors about ministry—in effect asking them to leave shore on a sailboat with you as you travel to a new place—you will increase the possibility of mutiny along the way. The church needs so much from its people right now. It needs a people who read the Bible in one hand and the newspaper in the other (to remember Karl Barth). It needs a people who are outgoing enough to demonstrate and talk about their faith in their daily lives. It needs a people who are generous with their resources and their emotions. It needs a people who will give some of their time to the institutional church's life (helping to lead worship and education and fellowship) but more of it to the world beyond the church's doors—living faithfully in the workplace, the marketplace and the home place, communicating clearly, serving others generously. These require a turning of some kind for most congregations. And they require good planning on our part.

My experience on *Azure Wind* reminded me of one thing and reaffirmed another. It reminded me that without flexibility our plans can become disastrous. More importantly, it reaffirmed the importance of good planning.

13

Jumping Ship

Who walked upon the foaming deep,
And calm amid its rage did sleep:

The return crossing from Isla Mujeres north to Galveston was filled with a sense of adventure. Our daily routines were joyfully interrupted whenever we encountered some other life. We saw a huge sea turtle on the second day, plodding along slowly but still fast enough that there wasn't time to go below and get my camera. On the fourth day, a huge pod of dolphins found the boat. The sounds of the engine and the bow breaking into the waves attracted them. They swam with the bow, and like cats nudging each other away from a bowl of food, they'd push each other away from bow and then circle around to have another turn at it.

Then, there were the birds. Not the big swimming birds. Not the ones that can drop down on the water, float a while and take off again, but swallows! Swallows who had no business being halfway across the gulf, which is where we first saw them. They'd fly toward the boat and circle slowly a couple of times. Then they'd fly a little closer and look for some safe place to land. You could tell they were exhausted, but wary. They'd hover and eventually they'd land. One of them landed on a crew member's head! Eventually they'd tuck themselves under the bimini or in some alcove...and rest...until it was time to take off again. It was a small, but enjoyable diversion. It's the birds by the way, that were the earliest navigation aids. Ever wonder how those Polynesian explorers found those small atolls in the vast Pacific ocean? They followed the birds that could be as far as two hundred miles away from their island nests!

There were several days coming home when the adventure grew with the seas. On the way over, we had used the autopilot for most of the time. We were moving into the wind and it was a great convenience to not have to sit at the helm all the time. We reclined in the cockpit seats and pushed buttons to adjust our course. On the way home, however, the winds came from behind us, which made the autopilot useless. We were in following seas which means that the stern of the boat is raised before the bow. And when it is raised by a stern-breaking wave, the boat wants to "round up", or turn toward that wave. The only way to keep moving forward is to disengage the autopilot and hand steer.

It's a rolly ride which became worse at night. For several days, as the afternoon sun set, the winds would begin to pick up. A ten knot breeze would develop into fifteen and twenty knots, and occasionally reach twenty-five. We reefed the mainsail, lowering it part way to keep the boat safe. The seas would grow and the ride would get worse and it was a challenge to hold a course and resist the boat's turning into the waves. In the dark, unable to see each approaching wave and steering by the compass made it all the more challenging. On one night watch, I was at the helm in just such fast seas, the boat pitching back and forth as a wave would pass rapidly under the hull. A fifteen degree heel to port became a fifteen degree heel to starboard in three seconds! I had trouble staying in the helm seat; I couldn't imagine trying to get much rest down below.

At that moment of high adventure (more accurately discomfort and stress), I remember thinking: *"Anybody want to jump ship?"* It never would have occurred to any of us to leave the boat. Or, to ask for a share of the life raft. In all my readings of high seas adventures, nobody leaves the boat willingly in the middle of a stormy sea. As long as the boat is not sinking, you don't leave, and if it is sinking, you leave together. There may be accidents or treachery, but not voluntary separation! If you are an unhappy member of the crew, you wait for the next port to find another boat.

There's something here for the church. To leave in the midst of a stormy season is foolish. For nearly thirty of the thirty-two years I've been a Minister of Word and Sacrament, the church has moved through stormy seas. Not all the time, but enough so that it gets wearisome. It's wearisome anticipating the next national meeting of my denomination because God continues to do interesting things at those meetings. God exposes people to a highly diverse church in a highly intense one-week meeting and the next thing you know those folks want to change their church. Then God takes the rest of the year (now two years) for the remainder of the church to evaluate that proposed change. If any proposal survives both the intense and the extended experiences, then we tend to trust it's something God wants us to honor. The rhythms of proposing and rejecting though, are wearying. Added to these national church meetings are the storms of reduced membership, reduced funding, reduced effectiveness at either making disciples or making a justice difference in the world. It's been a stormy season. Not the first in the church's history and not likely to be the last either.

But as far as I can tell, this denominational ship is still out at sea and floating. It hasn't reached a safe port yet. So, it'd be a really good idea to pause before jumping ship. Once overboard, there are no guarantees that anyone else will see you. You may wind up floundering in bitterness and abandonment and you may never find another boat for the rest of your faith journey.

14

Shedding

Every once in a while I go through a shedding moment. I want to simplify my life and usually begin by getting rid of unwanted possessions. I go through my clothes, our closets, the work shed, bookcases, and other hiding places. This usually frustrates my wife who never understands my timing. So on New Year's Day, while many are still sleeping and others are watching the parades on TV, and before the one football game that captures my interest, I shed. And I've learned to avoid certain locales in our home—the kitchen, the dining area side table, Marney's study. Much of what I shed I give away; some gets tossed.

I came back from my sailing voyage in a shedding mood. I felt the urge to simplify because I had been with people who have learned to live modestly. Some cruisers don't own anything other than what's on their boat. They've sold their home, car, furniture. Maybe they have put a few personal items in a storage locker somewhere. Whenever I visited one of the boats in the anchorage, I found myself looking for the owners' personal effects not essential to sailing: the embroidered sign, the few books, a photograph. There would always be a few things, but very few. The limited space on a sailboat necessitates shedding.

The same thing happened to my parents as they aged. They moved from a house to an apartment to a two bedroom condominium, to a one bedroom apartment, to a hospice hospital room. They shedded. In her hospice room, my mother's final possessions were a comfortable chair, a portable CD player, her stack of music CDs and about five framed pictures.

I once read that by the time we reach the end of our lives, all of our possessions should have a story attached to them. Otherwise, we ought to get rid of them. "So and so gave this to me." "I took this picture when I was on such and such trip." "I found this at the flea market back in 1952."

Fewer material possessions were not the only indicator of a modest life style. The cruisers I met lived by the sun's rising and setting. They were up early. They ate simply. They worked early and rested in the mid-day heat. They ran errands late in the day and didn't seem to mind the lack of conveniences to which we are so accustomed. No dishwashers, ice makers, no clothes washers on board.

Not all of us are meant to be sailors. But I suspect most of us would benefit by a periodic look around our lives with an eye to live a bit more simply. For those of us who claim the counsel of the Scriptures and a commitment to follow the lead of Jesus, we have lots of reasons to do so. Our culture and context make it hard, but it's not impossible.

Change something about how we eat, travel, work, serve. Turn our possessions into a great storybook. Resist increasing our financial debt. Live a bit more modestly.

Jesus instructed the seventy to travel lightly. I am glad for this reminder from my sailing friends, as if the Scriptures weren't reason enough.

15

Be Still and Know

There is a wonderful story in the Old Testament Scriptures about a man of faith who was facing a great challenge. Fearful, he ran away and hid in a cave. God called to him to come out and to face his challenge. In that moment the man was reminded that God was not in the whirlwind or the storm so much as in the silence. For in the quiet moment in his cave, the man still heard the voice of the One who had created and was accompanying him through life. In the quiet…

More than anything else, this time away on a sailboat has reminded me to be more quiet and less noisy with my life.

Oh, my time away was busy and filled with noise. It was a seven week adventure. I met a personal goal in sailing across the gulf. I spent my days in a very different routine. I learned a lot about boats, and people, and life on the water and along the shoreline.

Yet for all this noise, the quiet moments were the ones that brought a sense of peace and awareness of God's world. I'd sit in the early mornings at the marina and look out across the harbor, watching the birds, the iguanas and the sunrise. I'd stretch out on the bow and watch the boat move rhythmically through the waves. I'd close my eyes and listen for the simple noises of the sea. I'd taste a meal and wonder more than I ever have about the people and work that was reflected in the food in front of me.

In her book, <u>Dakota</u>, author Kathleen Norris writes about making silence together. For a classroom of children or a community of faith, such a goal requires everyone to join together in becoming still for a time. To marvel at the quiet and then to begin hearing the voice of the One who loves us so fully, the Word.

Be still and know…God's voice can be heard, speaking in the quiet, calling us out of our caves to face the challenges, the adventures, the opportunities to see God's world in a different and fresh way. And hearing that voice raises within us gratitude and hope: gratitude that we are not alone, gratitude for what is and hope for what is unfolding in front of us. God's purposes are being worked out through you and me.

APPENDIX A

Excerpts from the Log

Voyage of Azure Wind
February 28–April 15, 2006

January 29, 2006

One month away and an office move yet ahead. There is a growing sense of excitement and challenge in me. A dream is about to become real and I know that it won't unfold exactly as I have imagined it for the last eighteen months. But, it will happen and I am going to go sailing.

I am excited. I am getting ready. I am hopeful about what I'll learn of God's world, the sea, and myself.

Day 1—Tuesday, February 28, 2006

Tonight, many folks will be eating pancakes and other "fat" foods—preparing at least symbolically—for a season of simplicity, denial, preparation for the Easter feast! Not me, I'm the fool who wants to do something different, see things from a different perspective and hopefully gain insight and appreciation for God's complex and wonderful world.

So, off we go today on *Azure Wind.*

Day 2—Wednesday, March 1, 2006

We've made slow progress to the east—had to motor sail most of the night. Took the watch from 9–11 pm and 3–5 am; slept from 7–9, 11–3, and 5–8 am

The stars were bright and for a while we turned off the engine…I thought of Psalm 8 (O Lord Our Lord how majestic is your name in all the earth). It's a rare opportunity to experience God's creation from the view of the water—no land in sight…

It was reassuring that throughout the night we would see the lights of the oil and gas rigs. At one point, I saw a star that was so large and bright that I thought it was a single rig light—couldn't believe it when I realized it was not attached to the horizon. At another point I saw two sets of three lights flashing in sequence that made me think it was the bow and stern of a ship at anchor—not true. It was the three lights of a darkened oil rig and when we were close enough I could see the shadow of the rig outlined against the horizon with my binoculars. It's amazing how much you can see with your night vision…

I also thought about the planning it takes for a voyage—the detail, the variety of things to think about (the safety of the boat, the rigging and sails, the food, the creature comforts, the course planning, the learnings), AND the anxiety as the moment approaches that you first let go of land and make the commitment to leave….

Day 3—Thursday, March 2, 2006

Yesterday's sail was slow. We made 75 miles towards Isla (VMG = Velocity Made Good) in the first 24 hours. And we have made 158 miles to Isla as of 9:00 am this morning.

There are some clouds forming to the sourh and this may be a good sign for a little better weather.

I've finally got my sea legs and stomach. For the first two days I felt nauseous enough to know I wasn't at full speed. I had eaten small bits on and off, and yesterday, I had a sandwich for lunch and a half bowl of stew for supper. I've had bananas and granola bars and lots of water.

My parents are accompanying me on this trip. My Dad is with me because of a book Marney gave me. <u>Mudhouse Sabbath</u> is written by Lauren Winner raised Jewish who is now Christian. She writes about some of the traditions of keeping faith in the Jewish home—her book is about lifestyles and the spiritual disciplines—reading her book I'm struck that I learned much of that through my father's Jewish family—so I think of Dad as I travel. Mom is present through a Culligan water pitcher. After her death, I brought it home and put it on the boat, am using it to filter the water one more time.

Last night, on watch, I thought about the Christmas/Epiphany Hymn—*Watchman Tell us of the Night*—there the singing goes back and forth between a watchman and a traveler. It suggests they are different people. On a sailboat the watchman and traveler are one and the same. Maybe that's worth remembering in the church—we don't need pew sitters who are watchers—we need sailors who are travelers and watchmen/women both—moving toward a goal and looking for the encouraging signs up ahead.

Day 4—Friday, March 3, 2006

3:10 am—Friday morning—we're under sail, speed 3.2 knots, 27.30.05 N and 91.21.35W, we are 428 miles from Isla—which means we've gone 200 miles—about 1/3 of the way there—we've moved off the shelf, into deeper water, no more platforms, and there's one ship I'm tracking. Winds are coming on a beam reach (E, NE) we've made a turn in the weather, and I expect this weather to stay with us…coming over the port side—we're doing 3.0 knots and 3.0 VMG.

Yesterday (Thursday) we had 25 gallons of fuel remaining and another 7.5 gallons in gerry cans on the deck…calculating 0.4 gallons per hour of motoring—which is 80 hours of motoring or 250 miles range—not enough fuel to motor all the way.

Toward the end of the day, some dolphins came alongside the boat; and then at dusk began seeing the green phosphorescent plankton being disturbed by the boat's movement through the water.

No lights around, this is the first moment since we left, we are over the deep water of the gulf, on the edge of the continental shelf—what a great gift to make this trip.

Slept hard last night; Had some oatmeal for breakfast

Location at 9:30 am—27.14.7 N; 91.07.1 W

Day 5—Saturday, March 4, 2006

Friday was a tough day, I'm wearing thin with KC's criticisms. I face the very awkward situation where I'm the owner, the captain, but not the most experienced sailor on board…am tired of being told about all the things wrong with the boat. Yesterday, I felt my confidence begin to wane and my anxiety growing.

(Last night) keeping watch twice through the rolling and waves in darkness was confidence building. I'm better today (at 10:30 am) but I'm still on edge.

Day 6—Sunday, March 9, 2006

My devotions are concluded—and the reflections identified three impacts of this sabbatical leave for me: the importance of <u>worship</u>, and being part of a worshipping community, the need to be attentive to regular devotions and <u>journaling</u> (Marney and I covenanted to read Luke and Acts daily), and <u>patience</u> (I'm ready to get to Isla and it's (still) another three days).

After five days, I'm beginning to wonder if this sailing voyage may be the only long one in my life. I don't think I have the drive to learn all the skills I would want to have…I doubt (Marney and I) will be a cruising couple…AND I don't have it in me to keep up the hectic schedule that's involved in keeping the boat in Kemah.

…I know that there are trips and experiences still ahead for me—us. But even when my physical world begins to shrink I hope I will always keep looking for new things to do. I hope I will always remember to be curious about big things, happy in small things.

Day 7—Monday, March 10, 2006

4:30 am—bearing 142 degrees at speed of 3.5 knots, 108 miles from goal, stars bright and clear; coordinates: 23.21.7 N 87.52.0 W

There's some excitement building in me to sense we're getting close—to begin to think about seeing land—something of what other sailors have experienced

Some things that need to be done in Isla

1. resolve the battery charging problem

2. some air bubbles in the water pressure system

3. put a bolt through the stand for the wind charger (high)

4. good cleaning

5. fuel

Sunday afternoon…a surprise of a visit from a dolphin pod—about 40 of them and I took some good pictures. They played with the bow of the boat and it was a nice diversion in the empty sea…

Monday
The big surprise and bad news of the day is the batteries. After testing them, KC is pretty convinced we need a new set of four batteries. Today's work reminds me that good stewardship is an important part of this experience. We are so spoiled to have the electricity we have available to us. Sailors are measuring their use and consider management of electricity a critical issue…I'm more and more aware that stewardship implies (a) appreciation of the resources we have, (b) understanding of how best to use them, (c) managing the diversity of needs to work within a self-contained system.

Day 11, Friday March 10, 2006

Lots to tell since Sunday's entry…
   Final passage across was slow—we motored most of the way, the winds died about 100+ miles out…
Tuesday—arrived at Isla at 2 pm. **total trip time 6 days, 22 hours…**refueled the tank and began the check-in procedures into Mexico (Found the marina) Marina Paraiso—older, under re-construction from hurricane, 1 week cost = $192.00 (75 cents per foot per day)
Wednesday—went to Cancun…to get batteries, beer and water
Thursday—work day: emptied and cleaned bilge; finished repair on water pressure line; added 50 gallons of water with 5 gallon jugs; cleaned oil pan under diesel; fixed macerator in head; fixed holder for dinghy gas can; cleaned cockpit; cleaned galley
Friday—repaired sail (am waiting for arrival of new sail) and navigation planning for next leg to Belize (as I think ahead), I need to not

push schedule—don't sail unless you're comfortable and wait out the weather

Day 15—Tuesday, March 14, 2006

It's been a couple of days since I've written…

Saturday—said goodbye to first crew, Kevin and Bob; spent the day cleaning the boat and getting ready for the boys. Read some and then went to a Saturday night church service.

Met Pastor Gonzalez of the National Evangelical Presbyterian Church (don't know if this is connected to us or not). About 25 people attended a two hour service…Hardly understood a word but did recognize some of the music (thank God for a hymnody that bridges cultures)

The boys (Matt & Nick) were scheduled to arrive around 10:00–10:30 pm, but the plane was late so they made the last ferry over which came in at 12:30 pm. It was GREAT to see them. We stayed up until 1:30 am talking.

Sunday—a quiet beginning to the day; cooked breakfast of scrambled eggs and we got familiar with the boat. Changed out the headsail and made arrangements to do the mainsail on Monday. Went to town to watch Kansas and Texas play basketball. Then back to the boat by way of the grocery store. Grilled out on the boat and then talked and relaxed.

Monday—after the cruiser net news; Steve from Santih (Shawn-tee) came over and we looked at the mainsail Nick and Matt had brought. Bad news—wrong fit that might have been workable, BUT no grommets for reefing and Steve (a North Sails representa-tive) said it was not a good idea to have them installed here. Plus the sail was about 5.5 oz of Dacron instead of 7–9 oz Dacron. We began the search for a new mainsail and called home (ALSO FOUND OUT THAT GLOBALSTAR in MEXICO adds a roaming fee of $1.39 per minute—incredible—that about takes care of the cruising budget).

Tuesday morning—am thinking we'll sail to Puerto Morales for the customs check-in. Get there this afternoon, spend the evening on the boat, then the boys can snorkel while I do the customs thing in the morning and we'll sail back on Wednesday.

Day 18, Friday, March 17, 2006

(NOTE: *On Tuesday, we sailed to Puerto Moreles south of Cancun and sailed back on Wednesday, after registering the boat. The sail was a bit grueling, and we arrived at dusk avoiding the long reef that protects this town. Thank God Nick, who speaks Spanish, was with me on Wednesday. The sail home was less eventful.*)

Thursday—my life focused around saying goodbye to the boys. We went to Cancun by ferry. Nick left immediately for the airport; Matt and I went to the market and then had lunch.

Friday—I spent an hour getting ten gallons of water and then worked on the head. The macerator seems to be working fine when I remove the outflow line and let it drain. I'm pretty well convinced now that it works—a filthy job, though…oiled the wood today…am waiting for the customs person to take the official photograph of the boat and then I can go to town and look for bottled water and beer. There's a cruising community party tonight and I need to bring a dish to share—if I can figure something out.

Day 22, Tuesday, March 21, 2006

Yesterday was a good day. Kate arrived and after hearing the weather report, we made plans to stay on shore. The winds have remained high but there is a window coming on Wednesday and maybe Thursday to do some sailing.

Day 24, Thursday, March 23, 2006

Yesterday (Wednesday) was a day to sail. Kate, Peter (seminary friend) and I crossed the Cancun Channel several times and had an enjoyable time. Nothing spectacular, but simply decent winds, beautiful blue water and a reminder of why I love to sail.

I want to take a run at explaining why I'm planning to return early. (1) I was surprised by the number of problems that surfaced after the crossing (new batteries, mainsail problem, fresh water line, the macerator, oil in the bilge, fuel leak at the second filter on the engine, plus other issues). (2) The mainsail became a deal breaker. When I learned that it would take four to six weeks to have one made, I knew then that I didn't want to wait around for it (and gamble that it might not fit) and I don't want to go farther south and farther away from good services. (3) I put together a crazy schedule that did not account for repairs and bad weather. This meant that several people had to re-route their travels......I was into the hospitality and only worried about a timetable that looked like it would work on paper. (4) The cruising fund has been seriously depleted, between the repair costs, the travel adjustments and the cost of the marina. (5) I've not had the time to do enough reading and writing. Too many chores, not enough concentrated time and...I DO want to read. (6) My confidence was shaken a bit on the crossing from Galveston. Time plus new crew have done a lot to restore it, however.

Day 25, Friday, March 24, 2006

Yesterday, Kate, Peter, and I had a special outing to ChichenItza. We left around 8:15 am and headed to the Yucatan Peninsula. We rented a car and took the "free" road that brought us through several towns, lots of speed bumps and a few occasional sights.

The speed bumps are effective and unnerving. Most of them are marked, but not all. A few are worn down so as not to be potentially harmful, but the vast majority of them are the kind that will knock the shocks right off your wheel boots. We all pitched in to look for the bumps to help Peter, who drove.

We had heard about the cenotes (caverns with pools of water). At one site, there were steps leading down eighty feet underground into a cool, vast chamber of silence. It was especially impressive to learn that the Mayans used the underground river system that connects the cenotes for commerce.

From there we drove the final distance to ChichenItza. It is an impressive set of ruins. Once inside, we walked counter-clockwise from the main entrance—to the ball games, then the central castle, then down a long path to the sacrificial pool and back, and finally to the astrological observatory and several smaller areas. Most disturbing were the peddlers that laid their wares on blankets along the paths and persistently worked to distract you from this wonderful site. I hate being put in the "tourista" role.

Day 26, Saturday, March 25, 2006

Friday, the day after ChichenItza was spent doing odd chores, including making an inventory of the boat's food and other supplies. Then Kate and I walked to town, had some lunch, made a phone call, did some shopping and picked up some groceries before walking back. It was a good conversation with my daughter and the highlight of my week with her.

With each child I've had a great moment and that is clearly one of the highlights of this sabbatical: some renewal with my adult children.

After the cruiser's net this morning, Kate, Peter and I went to town to the cruisers' breakfast. I continue to be impressed by the variety of cruisers…some travel hard as long as the boat is working; others travel slow (some staying 1–2 years in a pleasant anchorage); still others travel infrequently as their boats permit. All travel with respect to the weather. Few boats venture out into winds predicting 20 knots or more. They want the traveling to be as easy as possible. And schedules get thrown away. As Bill on *Skol* said to me, I say to my friends—You can choose when to meet the boat, or where to meet the boat—but you can't choose both.

Then it was time to take Kate to Cancun for her return trip home. Sad to see her go.

Day 27, Sunday, March 26, 2006

We joined Bill and Susie (cruising couple friends on their fifty-eight foot boat, *Skol*) and attended the Catholic Church for worship. The service was lectionary based and the "less formal" mass was used. The only musical instrument was a guitar but the children's choir was wonderful. The other children sat in the front pews, girls on one side, boys on the other. Several adult women stood in the aisles by the children keeping an eye on them. Parents, families and older folks sat on the far sides and in the back. I was glad to be in a worshipping community for a few minutes.

Day 30, Wednesday, March 29, 2006

Yesterday was a great day…Marney arrived!

    Today…Just another day in paradise…

Day 32, Friday, March 31, 2006

Yesterday, we sailed to Isla Contoy, a national bird sanctuary northwest of Isla Mujeres. Took about four hours to get there. We sailed around the lighthouse at the northern tip of the island and then down the shallow inland waters to the bay where the national park offices are located. Grabbed a mooring ball and then visited the island. Good fun to walk around and see the birds.

This morning, we sailed back to Isla on the inside channel of the reef. It was a great sail with a stop to snorkel. Made good time home and then joined the cruising community for a potluck dinner and jam session with guitars, drums, kazoos, and conch shells!

Tomorrow (Saturday, April 1), Peter's wife, Donna joins us for a reunion from our first charter (in Guadeloupe, eastern Caribbean). Looking forward to being with good friends.

Day 38, Thursday, April 6, 2006

Said goodbye to Marney (Peter and Donna left yesterday). Greeted the arriving crew members for the crossing home.

Day 41, Sunday, April 9, 2006

We're heading north to Galveston on this Sunday morning, Palm Sunday. Yesterday, our final day ashore was OK. I sensed within me that it was time to make this crossing and waited for weather information that would confirm our window to proceed. I worked on electronics management. Cruising friend John came by and we reviewed the battery configuration; it is not as bad as I feared. We'll be fine working our way home. Picked up the weather report by e-mail which confirmed that today is the day to leave.

At 9:30 we backed *Azure Wind* out of the slip, raised the main and motored past the north point of Isla. The systems all look good, including the navigation program. I'm confident that we'll be OK, even if the ride gets to be a bit rough. Our plan is to motor north past Isla Contoy and then head northwest in order to catch the winds. We'll "clock" with the winds (turn the boat clockwise as the winds turn) and hope to keep our heading as close to the rhumb line (direct line home) as possible.

Day 42, Monday, April 10, 2006

At 9:05 am our position is: 22–24.09 N and 87–31.47 W

Yesterday was a bit stressful for a first day out. After the Isla Contoy waypoint, we tried to go northwest to Galveston, but we were heading straight into the wind. So we traveled west across the top of the Yucatan peninsula for several hours and then tacked to the north/east. And back west again. Slow going. Twenty-four hours later, we had traveled 85 miles toward our goal, having motor-sailed twenty hours, using precious fuel.

Day 44, Wednesday, April 12, 2006

We're now less than 300 miles to home; we're motor sailing and I'm feeling pretty tired and frustrated. It is uncomfortable to cook meals in a rolling sea. One crew member refused my advice to wear a seasickness patch…and got sick the first day out…has been laying in the cockpit twenty-four hours a day. It's added more work for the rest of us…

Just finished doing some chart work and learned that we had a 130-mile day on Monday-Tuesday from 4pm to 4pm…awesome! We're motor-sailing to keep up the five knot minimum speed

which, if we do so, will get us into Galveston on Friday evening
around 9pm and into the marina around midnight

Estimated: 300 miles in 60 hours from now

Day 46, Friday, April 14, 2006

Last night was a nightmare when we averted a disaster with the help
of two commercial vessels. We were heading into a tow line ten
thousand meters in length: six miles between the towing vessel and
the barge.

This morning, at 9:30 am, we're less than 75 miles from the Fuel
Dock in Galveston (add another 20 to get to Kemah)...almost
home.

This adventure is ending and there is some sadness in me. I may
never get to see the ocean so closely again. I'm ready to get off the
boat for a while—the constant movement is a reminder of how
important it is to rest and be still and how hard that is when the
earth (or water) beneath you is moving all the time. So, I'll be glad
to be still for a couple of weeks—at least at some various moments.

I've learned so much and...I've enjoyed nearly every part of this
journey and now want the time to process it all.

It's Good Friday, and I've missed being with the community of
faith this week. I valued gatherings for worship and remembering
and reflecting together on the gift of faith in Christ. Keep me
focused on today—not remorseful about the past nor anxious about
the future, but glad to look for God in the midst of the present...

*(Azure Wind arrived in Galveston at 10:30 pm on Friday evening,
having sailed through the jetty in increasing winds, dodging a half
dozen anchored ships plus a variety of commercial vessels moving into
and out of Bolivar Roads. After a brief clearance procedure with U.S.
Customs, we completed the voyage by sailing to Kemah, securing lines to*

*the dock slip at Marina del Sol at 4:00 am on Saturday, April 15,
2006.)*

APPENDIX B

Weather Forecast

April 9–15, 2006
Passage: Isla Mujeres to Galveston

One newer navigational aide is a company of meteorologists who study weather charts for sailors. For a fee, they will evaluate the weather forecast and identify a route with estimates of the direction of the wind for each six hour period, the projected speed, and at 7am each day, a latitude and longitude position. This is the e-mail I received. The projection called for a shift in the winds on Sunday that did not happen until later on Monday. The winds were a bit stiffer than projected which made for a fast ride home.

To: Dave Wasserman on SV "Azure Wind"
From: Commanders' Weather Corporation
Area: Isla Mujeres, Mx to Galveston, Tx
Departure: 0700CDT Sunday, April 9
Prepared: 1145CDT Saturday, April 8, 2006

Summary:

1. Cold front currently extends from the Carolinas SW to near Tampico, Mexico and is moving to the ESE

2. This frontal boundary will be approaching Isla Mujeres from the W Sunday morning and pass through the area Sunday afternoon/evening

3. A couple of weak low pressure waves may form on the front during Sunday slowing its forward speed

4. Front may kick off some shower activity, maybe a squall, but it appears that most of the activity will occur N of 22–24n and E of 85–86w

5. S to SW winds will be light ahead of this front, generally less than 15 kts

6. Winds shift into the NW behind the front and freshen into the teens

7. Sunday night and Monday, winds turn right to N and NE

   a. NE winds may increase to 20–25 kts Monday afternoon

8. Large ridge of high pressure will extend from New England SW to the W Gulf of Mexico

9. This will ridge will dominate the weather into Thursday

10. High pressure will settle over the N central Gulf of Mexico Friday morning and then retreats off to the E during Friday and Saturday

11. This will keep a general ENE to ESE wind generally in the teens Tuesday through Thursday

12. As the high moves off to the E, winds in the W Gulf will turn right to SSE Friday

13. SSE winds will freshen to 16–22 kts Saturday ahead of an approaching cold front from the W

Routing

1. Have you heading N out of Isla Mujeres for 12–18 hours with SSE to SW winds

2. Then, turn NW as winds shift into the N and NE behind the cold front and follow a rhumb line to Galveston

3. Please see waypoints in the wind forecast

Wind forecast

Wind directions are TRUE, wind speed in KTS, and time is CDT

Sun, Apr 9

07: 190–210/ 8–15 depart
13: 260–280/ 6–12
19: 310–330/13–20
Weather: Variable clouds with chance of a few scattered showers, maybe a squall
Seas: 3–5 ft SSE swell becoming 5–7 ft NNW swell at night

Mon, Apr 10

01: 330–350/12–18 heading NW
07: 010–030/13–20 nr 22 55n/87 05w
13: 030–050/15–20
19: 030–050/18–25
Weather: Partly cloudy
Seas: 4–7 ft NNW-NNE swell

Tue, Apr 11

01: 060–080/18–25
07: 060–080/15–20 nr 24 10n/88 30w
13: 060–080/ 8–15
19: 060–080/12–18
Weather: Fair
Seas: 3–5 ft NE swell

Wed, Apr 12

07: 080–100/15–20 nr 25 55n/90 20w
19: 060–080/10–17
Weather: Fair
Seas: 3–5 ft ENE swell

Thu, Apr 13

07: 090–110/10–15 nr 27 20/92w
19: 100–120/12–17
Weather: Fair to partly cloudy
Seas: 2–4 ft E swell

Fri, Apr 14

07: 150–170/ 8–15 nr 28 50/93 55w
19: 160–180/10–17 nr Galveston
Weather: Partly cloudy
Seas: 2–4 ft ESE swell

Sat, Apr 15—vicinity of Galveston

07: 170–190/ 8–15
19: 160–180/16–22

Weather: Partly cloudy
Seas: building to 4–7 ft SE swell

Best Regards,

Dave P (meteorologist)

About "Azure Wind"

We named our boat *Azure Wind* for several reasons. The "A" and the "W" have roots in our family names. Giving the wind a color drew us to those special Caribbean sailing places we've known where the turquoise blue is so brilliant and rich in tone. We've come to recognize an azure wind anywhere that blue meets blue, from sky to water, and creates a setting for peace and spiritual renewal.

978-0-595-40512-1
0-595-40512-6

Printed in the United States
58783LVS00001B/86